Sally O. Lee's
Book of Cats

Sally O. Lee's **Book of Cats**

I would like to thank my family and friends
for their love and support in helping
me to write and publish this book.

Library of Congress Control Number: 2015902875

For more information: visit www.sallyleebooks.com
Sally O. Lee's Book of Cats/ Sally O. Lee

Summary: This is a compilation of Sally O. Lee's cat illustrations.

ISBN-13: 978-1508525882

ISBN-10: 1508525889

This book is typeset in Garamond.
The illustrations are rendered in various mediums including watercolor,
pen and ink, pencil, pen and digital.

Printed in the U.S.A.

First Edition

To:

My yoga pals who teach me how
to not take myself too seriously.

And to my little pal, Dominic.
I love you to the moon and back.

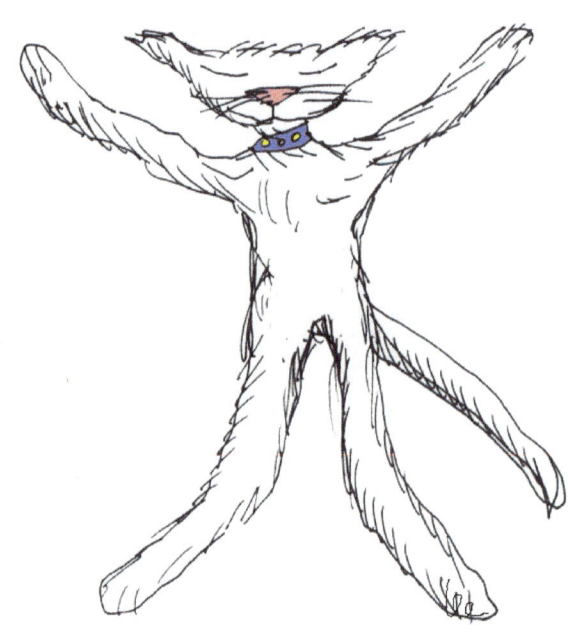

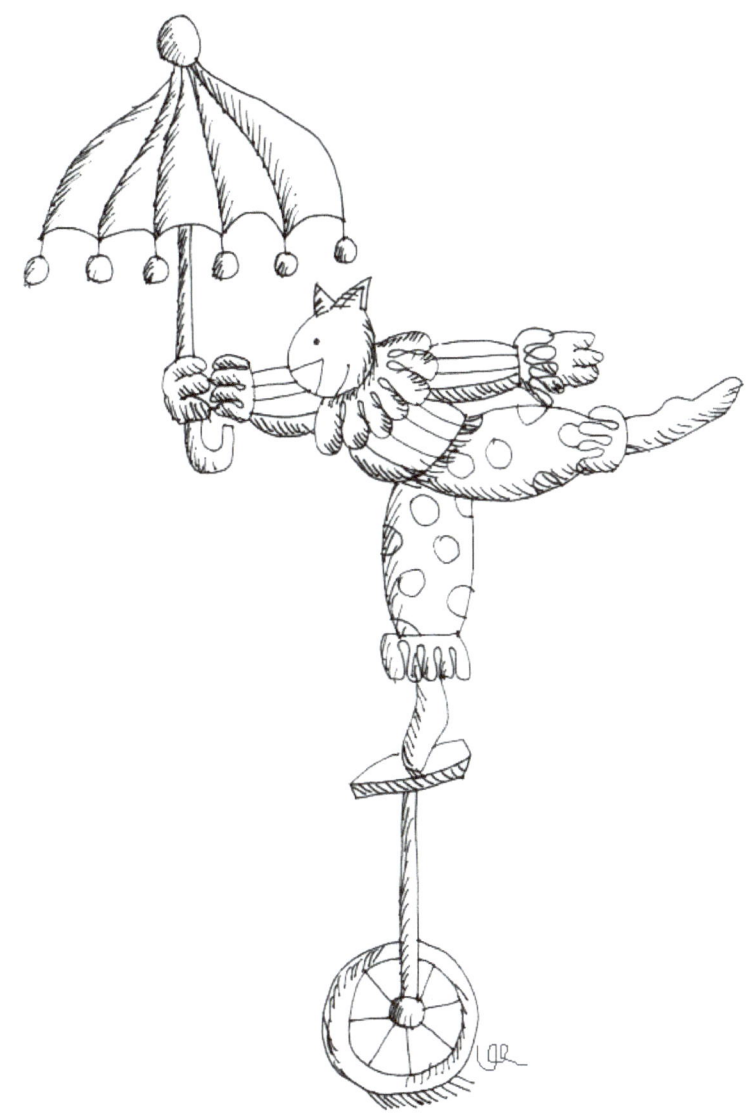

Happy Halloween!